Building an Igloo

Text and Photographs by

Building an Igloo

Ulli Steltzer

SQUARE
FISH

Henry Holt and Company
New York

for ⊃ᑭᕐ ᑭᓴᕐ   ᑭᒡᒍᑕᕐ

and for Jennifer, Paul Jonas, Eli, and Benjamin

SQUARE
FISH

An Imprint of Macmillan
175 Fifth Avenue
New York, NY 10010
mackids.com

Library of Congress Cataloging-in-Publication Data
Steltzer, Ulli.
Building an igloo / by Ulli Steltzer
1. Inuit—Dwellings—Juvenile literature. 2. Igloos—Juvenile literature.
[1. Igloos. 2. Inuit—Dwellings. 3. Eskimos—Dwellings.] I. Title.
E99.E7S8235   1995   693'.91'089971—dc20   95-5893
ISBN 978-0-8050-6313-4

Originally published in the United States by Henry Holt and Company
First Square Fish Edition: April 2013
Square Fish logo designed by Filomena Tuosto

20 19 18 17 16 15 14 13 12
LEXILE: 720L

Winter in the Northern Arctic is long and cold—so long that by September the ocean starts to freeze over, and so cold that the ice soon forms a cover six and a half feet deep. No wonder, then, that any moisture in the air freezes right away. On cloudy days it may come down as snow; on clear days the air is full of tiny, silvery ice crystals. A new layer of white covers land and sea every day, packing down hard in some places and settling loosely in others.

Trees have never grown in this part of the world. For centuries the people of the Arctic, the Inuit, built their houses of snow. They called them "igloo" in some regions, "igluviak" in others. Snow was everywhere, and the only tool needed was a knife of bone, antler, or walrus tusk.

Depending on the size of a family, its igloo was big or small. Even giant igloos were built as places to dance to the sound of drums. Both light and heat were provided by a stone lamp (called a "kuliq") burning seal fat and using the cotton-like seeds of a small plant for a wick. Of course, each igloo needed a chimney where hot air could escape, or the whole top would begin to melt and might cave in on the people.

When many people lived in an igloo, they sometimes damaged its walls. Rather than continually patching their igloo, the family would build a new one. Often an igloo was abandoned because the family moved to better hunting grounds, leaving their old house to melt away in the summer sun.

Tookillkee Kiguktak lives in Griese Fiord, the most northern settlement in Canada, on Ellesmere Island. He does not live in an igloo; like all the Inuit of today, he lives in a house. But when Tookillkee was a little child, he lived in an igloo, and when he was a boy he learned how to build one. Ever since, when he goes hunting far away for a musk ox or a polar bear, he builds an igloo for shelter.

A hunter never goes alone on a long trip. Tookillkee likes to take along Jopee, one of his four sons, and of course Jopee—like his father—long ago learned how to build an igloo.

It takes several hours of hard work to build a good igloo. The most important thing is to find the right kind of snow. Not too soft, not too hard.

Tookillkee starts walking over the land. Only when the surface remains unbroken under his feet does he stop. With his carpenter saw he checks the depth and quality of the snow. On a rocky slope, like the site shown here, he has to be especially careful to find a large enough area of good snow. Once he has found it, he steps to one side of the good snow and paces off a circle. This is where he will build his igloo.

Tookillkee outlines the blocks in the snow before he cuts them. Then, with the blade of the saw, he lifts up each one. It can weigh from eighteen to twenty-seven pounds depending on size. He lines up the blocks alongside the growing trench from which they were cut.

When he has cut all the blocks, it is time to start building the igloo.

He cuts diagonally into the blocks to start a spiral.

Jopee helps with the carrying. Before bringing a fresh block, he waits until his father has set the last one in position.

After setting each block, Tookillkee trims and cleans its surface with a long knife.

The final blocks that round off the top need skillful shaping and fitting.

Tookillkee reaches up and places the last block, the keystone of the igloo. He is locked in.

With his knife he cuts a low doorway and crawls out.

After the two men fill in the cracks with the soft snow from the undercut side of the blocks, Tookillkee builds a chimney.

Then he cuts a window in the front, above the entrance. He has chosen a piece of ice from the ocean for a windowpane. It gives much light to the inside, a strange blue-green light like that surrounding a swimmer under water.

Tookillkee decides to build a porch. It will keep the cold draft from coming inside and will give him storage space, especially for food, boots, and bulky clothing. He cuts more snow blocks. After attaching the first two rows to both sides of the igloo's entrance, he rounds off the top on the gentle slope of a spiral. No chimney is needed for the porch, and the cracks are filled in quickly.

The igloo is ready.

It is evening. Father and son settle down inside. They look out on the frozen ocean. Tomorrow will be a day of hunting.